All of the happy animals in this book
live now (or once did) at Farm Sanctuary,
a shelter for farm animals, where their
only job is to enjoy life and be loved.

OUR FARM

BY THE ANIMALS OF FARM SANCTUARY

poems by Maya Gottfried

paintings by Robert Rahway Zakanitch

Alfred A. Knopf   New York

MAYA

Miss GRandMAMa Moo

Wisdom
by Maya, a cow

My name is Maya,
but you can call me "Grandmama Moo."
Because, my dear, I was here before you!

Come walk with me, darling,
little calf, little one.
I'll show you the most wonderful spot in the sun.

And the sweetest patch of grass.
And the softest bed of clover.

Come here now, baby,
let Grandmama Moo
teach you a wise old thing or two.

M A Y FLY

CLUCK

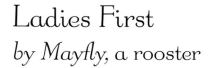

Ladies First
by *Mayfly*, a rooster

I'm the first to wake in the morning
    and the first to sense the coming storm.
I keep an eye on all of the hens
    and make sure that they are safe.
I stand guard from my post on the fence
    as they scratch, scratch, scratch and bathe in the dust.
Please step aside for the chickens.
    A true rooster knows: it is always ladies first.

Freedom!
by J.D., a piglet

I'm free!
And I'm running, and I'm running,
and oh, I can feel the sun on my snout.
There goes a fence post!
And I'm running, and I'm running,
and oh, the mud is spraying on my warm belly
           so cool,
             and wet.
There goes a tree!
And I'm running, and I'm running,
and oh! I hear the wind
           whistling
           in my ears.
There's that person who feeds me.
And I'm running, and I'm running,
and . . . wait!
That person who feeds me?!
I'll run later. . . .

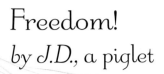

kari

cluck

oink cluck

cluck

cluck

JD Piglet

Different
by Gabriella, a bantam chicken

I like to strut. She likes to shimmy.
            He likes to take in the view.
We're all different, but we're still related,
            and in some ways
                        just
                                    like
                                                you.

Wandering
by Clarabell, a goat

Dah-ah-ah-ah-arling,
this is my home.
Wherever my mind wanders
is exactly where I roam.

Daisies, they call to me.
Trees sing my name.
So I follow their invitations
and go where I may.

...CLUCK

clarabell

We Are Family
by the ducklings

Look here!
Can I follow it?
—*Prince Cornwall*

Wriggle, wriggle,
splash!
—*Princess Charmaine*

U C K L I N G S

Brother,
watch me swim.
—Poppy Seed

Sister,
shake a tail!
—Sesame Seed

Ramsey

Our Introduction
by Ramsey, a sheep

Don't make a move.
I haven't decided whether you are to be trusted.
You don't look like my other sheep friends.
I'll have to think this over.

Hmmm.
Nice and gentle. Not too pushy.
Yes, I think you pass inspection.
Just mind your manners, kiddo.

Now that we've come to an understanding,
I suppose you could rub my nose.
Thanks.
And if you happen to have a carrot,
I might even call you pal.

Dance
by Whisper, a turkey

See our magnificent
dance
in
the
grass.

We are so graceful,
like
a
ballet
class.

B

The Hill
by Bonnie, a donkey

here
the fields and trees
the wide green hills
all in front of me

here
my mane swept by wind
here
my ears filled with quiet

why ever stray?
i'd rather be here
watch the land
feel the sun

A Flower's Life
by *Violet, a pig*

My name is Violet, and I am a flower.

See:

My bed is made of grass.
My hooves are planted firmly in the dirt.
I perk up like a daffodil after it rains.
And I smell sweet, like a lily.
(I take a sunbath nearly every day!)

I must be a flower.
Truly.

Now, if you'll excuse me, I'm going to roll in the mud.

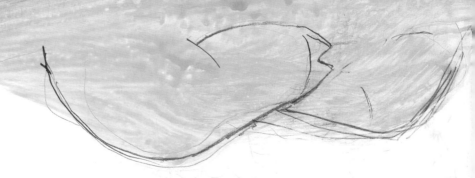

ioLet

sniff

A R i

It's Good to Be a Kid
by Ari and Alicia, the baby goats

Hello there!
How are you?

Cool bag.
Let's have a sample.

Yummy pants leg.
　　　Can I try some?

I'd like to nibble on your sleeve.
　　　Nice shoes, do they taste good?

Nice to meet

　　　chew.

WHITAK

Afraid?
by *Whitaker, a calf*

Really?
You're afraid of . . . me?

When I grow up, I'll be big and strong,
but I won't be . . . mean.

I was hoping that we would be friends.
We could run through the great field . . . together!

Why don't you think it over?
I'll be right over there with the . . . ladybugs.

Follow My Lead!
by Diego, a duck

Quack!
Yes, quack!
Are you ready?
Come along with me now.
Join my parade!

Okay!
Everyone into the water.
Flap, flap go our feet.
Keep an eye on my tail feathers.
Follow my lead!

Right, next up the bank!
Let's march, my friends.
Step one.
Shake two.
Waddle three.
And quack!

Oh, yes!
Quack!

Diego

Haikus
by the rabbits

I'm very nervous.
A noise back there! Must. Keep. Still.
When it's safe, I'll run.
—Cece

BArnaby

See me in the grass?
Maybe I will hop to food . . .
Or go sniff pansies.
—Barnaby

Thank You
by *Hilda*, a sheep

Thank you to the wind that cools
Thank you to the moonbeams that shine
Thank you to the field of wheat
and to the soft grass below
Thank you to the sunflowers that sway
Thank you to the sky above
Thank you to the kind hearts and hands
that brought me to my home

Hilda

Farm Sanctuary: A Note for Grown-ups

Picture a place where cows graze in fields, pigs play in snow, chickens stretch their wings in the sun, and ducks swim together happily. This is the image most of us have of farm life. But sadly, the vast majority of farm animals in the United States are not living in such idyllic conditions. They are usually housed in huge, crowded facilities where they are denied the wind, the sun, the green grass, and the warm dirt that they love.

Enter Farm Sanctuary. Founded in 1986, Farm Sanctuary provides shelter for neglected and abused farm animals. Whether a pig from a small farm that has been denied proper nutrition, a sheep that has been left for dead in a stockyard, or a chick that has been discarded by a factory farm, Farm Sanctuary speaks for those who cannot speak for themselves.

Led by cofounder and president Gene Baur, Farm Sanctuary has threefold intentions: rescue, education, and advocacy. In the decades since its inception, Farm Sanctuary has saved thousands of animals and educated millions of people. Farm Sanctuary is also a primary advocate behind important legislation and policies that protect and promote compassion for farm animals in the United States. In 2008 it was a driving force behind Proposition 2, groundbreaking legislation in California that banned three of the cruelest confinement systems used in farming (battery cages, veal crates, and gestation crates).

Farm Sanctuary is a national organization with two spacious farms, near Orland, California, and Watkins Glen, New York. I've volunteered for Farm Sanctuary in New York City and visited the New York farm a number of times, and during those visits I've had the pleasure of meeting many of the wonderful animal residents and people there. Since I was young, I've considered myself an animal lover, but because of Farm Sanctuary I've had the privilege of truly getting to know many cows, chickens, goats, and other farm animals as the individuals they are. I've tried to capture both the personalities of the animals and the loving, peaceful spirit of the place in these poems.

If you would like to learn more about Farm Sanctuary or plan your own visit, please go to www.farmsanctuary.org.

With peace to all beings,
Maya Gottfried

Acknowledgments

Thank you to Nancy Siscoe for open-minded oversight and editing.

Thank you to the people of Farm Sanctuary: to Gene Baur, Cofounder
and President, for listening to and having faith in my ideas; to Tricia Barry,
Communications Director, for meeting with and trusting me; to Natalie Bowman,
Communications Manager, for sensitive commentary and warm hospitality;
to Susie Coston, National Shelter Director, for precious feedback and positive support.

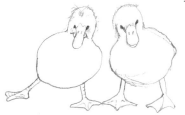

Thank you to Aimee Hartmann, who introduced me to Farm Sanctuary,
and offered me a ride for my very first visit. I will never forget the sweet din
of chirping baby chicks rising from the backseat.
—Maya Gottfried

Thanks to Nancy Siscoe, who is the absolute best; thanks to Sarah Hokanson for yet
another beautifully designed book; thanks to Jane Lahr, who is there when you need her.
—Robert Rahway Zakanitch

THIS IS A BORZOI BOOK PUBLISHED BY ALFRED A. KNOPF
Text copyright © 2010 by Maya Gottfried
Illustrations copyright © 2010 by Robert Rahway Zakanitch
All rights reserved. Published in the United States by Alfred A. Knopf, an imprint of Random House Children's Books,
a division of Random House, Inc., New York.
Knopf, Borzoi Books, and the colophon are registered trademarks of Random House, Inc.
Visit us on the Web! www.randomhouse.com/kids
Educators and librarians, for a variety of teaching tools, visit us at www.randomhouse.com/teachers

Library of Congress Cataloging-in-Publication Data
Gottfried, Maya.
Our farm : by the animals of Farm Sanctuary / Maya Gottfried, Robert Rahway Zakanitch. — 1st ed.
p. cm.
ISBN 978-0-375-86118-5 (trade) — ISBN 978-0-375-96118-2 (lib. bdg.)
1. Domestic animals—Juvenile poetry. 2. Livestock—Juvenile poetry. 3. Farm Sanctuary (Watkins Glen, N.Y.)—Juvenile poetry.
4. Children's poetry, American. I. Zakanitch, Robert. II. Farm Sanctuary (Watkins Glen, N.Y.). III. Title.
PS3607.O87O87 2010
811'.6—dc22
2009014885

The illustrations in this book were created using watercolors, pencil, and ink.

MANUFACTURED IN CHINA   February 2010
10 9 8 7 6 5 4 3 2 1   First Edition
Random House Children's Books supports the First Amendment and celebrates the right to read.